Contents

5

16

25

39

46

D0503438

peanut butter-chocolate trifle

PREP: 20 min. | MAKES: 12 servings, ⅔ cup each.

▸ what you need!

1 pkg. (3.9 oz.) JELL-O Chocolate Instant Pudding

1 pkg. (3.4 oz.) JELL-O Vanilla Flavor Instant Pudding

3 cups cold milk, divided

¼ cup PLANTERS Creamy Peanut Butter

1 tub (8 oz.) COOL WHIP Whipped Topping, thawed, divided

30 CHIPS AHOY! Cookies, chopped

3 Tbsp. chocolate syrup

▸ make it!

EMPTY dry pudding mixes into separate medium bowls. Add 1½ cups milk to each; beat with whisk 2 min. Add peanut butter to vanilla pudding; beat until well blended. Stir ½ cup COOL WHIP into pudding in each bowl.

SPOON chocolate pudding mixture into 2-qt. serving bowl; cover with layers of half each of the remaining COOL WHIP and chopped cookies. Repeat layers, using vanilla pudding mixture.

DRIZZLE with syrup.

SPECIAL EXTRA:
Top chocolate pudding layer with 2 sliced bananas before covering with remaining layers as directed.

MAKE AHEAD:
Prepare trifle as directed but do not top with syrup. Refrigerate up to 6 hours. Drizzle with syrup just before serving.

sundae cheesecake bars

PREP: 15 min. (plus baking and refrigerating) | **MAKES:** 30 servings.

▸ what you need!

9 HONEY MAID Honey Grahams, finely crushed (about 1½ cups)

3 Tbsp. butter, melted

2 pkg. (8 oz. each) PHILADELPHIA Cream Cheese, softened

⅓ cup sugar

½ cup BREAKSTONE'S or KNUDSEN Sour Cream

¼ cup milk

1 pkg. (3.4 oz.) JELL-O Vanilla Flavor Instant Pudding

2 eggs

1½ cups COOL WHIP Whipped Topping (Do not thaw.)

4 squares BAKER'S Semi-Sweet Chocolate, chopped

1 square BAKER'S White Chocolate

12 maraschino cherries, drained, chopped

¼ cup chopped PLANTERS Pecans

▸ make it!

HEAT oven to 350°F.

MIX graham crumbs and butter until well blended; press onto bottom of 13×9-inch pan. Bake 5 min.

BEAT cream cheese and sugar with mixer until well blended. Add sour cream and milk; mix well. Blend in dry pudding mix. Add eggs, 1 at a time, mixing on low speed after each just until blended. Spread over crust.

BAKE 30 min. or until center is almost set. Run knife around edge to loosen from pan; cool.

MICROWAVE COOL WHIP and chopped chocolate on HIGH 1½ min. or until chocolate is melted, stirring after 1 min. Cool 15 min. Meanwhile, melt white chocolate as directed on package.

SPREAD COOL WHIP mixture over cheesecake; top with cherries and nuts. Drizzle with melted white chocolate. Refrigerate 1 hour.

5

floating fruit parfaits

PREP: 15 min. (plus refrigerating) | **MAKES:** 6 servings.

▶ what you need!

½ cup sliced fresh strawberries

¾ cup boiling water

1 pkg. (0.3 oz.) JELL-O Strawberry Flavor Sugar Free Gelatin

½ cup cold water

¾ cup ice cubes

1 cup plus 6 Tbsp. thawed COOL WHIP LITE Whipped Topping, divided

▶ make it!

SPOON berries into 6 parfait or dessert glasses. Add boiling water to dry gelatin mix in medium bowl; stir 2 min. until completely dissolved. Add cold water and ice cubes; stir until ice is melted. Pour ¾ cup gelatin over berries. Refrigerate 20 min. or until gelatin is set but not firm.

ADD 1 cup COOL WHIP to remaining gelatin; whisk until well blended. Spoon over gelatin in glasses.

REFRIGERATE 1 hour or until firm. Serve topped with remaining COOL WHIP.

VARIATION:
Prepare as directed, using JELL-O Orange Flavor Sugar Free Gelatin and substituting cantaloupe balls for the strawberries.

SPECIAL EXTRA:
Add ½ cup seedless grapes with the strawberries.

STORING FRESH FRUIT:
Most fruits keep best when stored in the refrigerator. Berries, cherries and plums should not be washed before refrigeration, since excess moisture will cause these fruits to spoil more quickly.

JELL-O magic mousse

▶ what you need!

- 3 cups boiling water
- 1 pkg. (6 oz.) JELL-O Gelatin, any red flavor
- 1 tub (16 oz.) COOL WHIP Whipped Topping, thawed, divided

▶ make it!

ADD boiling water to dry gelatin mix in medium bowl; stir 2 min. until completely dissolved. Reserve 1 cup COOL WHIP; refrigerate. Whisk remaining COOL WHIP into gelatin until well blended. (Mixture will be thin.)

POUR into 1½-qt. glass bowl or 10 glasses.

REFRIGERATE 8 hours or until firm. Top with reserved COOL WHIP just before serving.

SUBSTITUTE:
Prepare using any flavor JELL-O Gelatin.

SUBSTITUTE:
Prepare using 2 pkg. (3 oz. each) JELL-O Gelatin.

Layered Desserts & Parfaits

7

caramel apple dessert

PREP: 15 min. (plus refrigerating) | MAKES: 16 servings.

▶ what you need!

60 NILLA Wafers, finely crushed (about 2 cups)

⅓ cup butter, melted

1 pkg. (8 oz.) PHILADELPHIA Cream Cheese, softened

¼ cup sugar

3¼ cups milk, divided

1 tub (8 oz.) COOL WHIP Whipped Topping, thawed, divided

2 pkg. (3.4 oz. each) JELL-O Vanilla Flavor Instant Pudding

½ cup caramel ice cream topping, divided

1 each red and green apple, chopped

¼ cup PLANTERS COCKTAIL Peanuts, chopped

▶ make it!

MIX wafer crumbs and butter; press onto bottom of 13×9-inch pan. Beat cream cheese, sugar and ¼ cup milk with mixer until well blended. Stir in 1 cup COOL WHIP; spread over crust.

BEAT dry pudding mixes and remaining milk with whisk 2 min. Stir in ¼ cup caramel topping. Spoon over cream cheese layer; top with remaining COOL WHIP.

REFRIGERATE 5 hours or until firm. Top with apples, nuts and remaining caramel topping just before serving.

KEEP APPLES FROM TURNING BROWN:
After cutting the apples, minimize browning by dipping them in 1 cup water mixed with 1 Tbsp. lemon juice before adding to dessert.

chilly chocolate-mint parfaits

PREP: 15 min. (plus refrigerating) | **MAKES:** 4 servings.

▶ what you need!

1 pkg. (1 oz.) JELL-O Chocolate Flavor Fat Free Sugar Free Instant Pudding

2 cups cold fat-free milk

Few drops peppermint extract

Few drops green food coloring

1 cup thawed COOL WHIP Sugar Free Whipped Topping

2 packs (0.81 oz. each) NABISCO 100 CAL OREO Thin Crisps, coarsely broken

▶ make it!

BEAT first 3 ingredients with whisk 2 min. Refrigerate 10 min.

STIR food coloring into COOL WHIP. Layer half each of the pudding, COOL WHIP and OREO Crisps pieces in 4 (10-oz.) parfait glasses. Repeat layers of pudding and COOL WHIP.

REFRIGERATE 30 min. Sprinkle with remaining OREO Crisps pieces just before serving.

SPECIAL EXTRA:
Sprinkle 1 small crushed candy cane evenly over parfaits just before serving.

Layered Desserts & Parfaits

JELL-O chocolate-peanut butter parfaits

PREP: 10 min. (plus refrigerating) | MAKES: 6 servings.

▸ what you need!

- 1 pkg. (3.9 oz.) JELL-O Chocolate Instant Pudding
- 2 cups plus 3 Tbsp. cold milk, divided
- 3 Tbsp. PLANTERS Creamy Peanut Butter
- 1 cup thawed COOL WHIP Whipped Topping

▸ make it!

BEAT dry pudding mix and 2 cups milk with whisk 2 min.; set aside. Gradually add remaining milk to peanut butter in medium bowl, stirring with whisk until well blended. Stir in COOL WHIP.

SPOON half the pudding evenly into 6 parfait glasses; top with layers of peanut butter mixture and remaining pudding.

REFRIGERATE 30 min.

peach & raspberry trifle

▶ what you need!

- 3 Tbsp. orange juice
- ¼ tsp. almond extract
- 1 pkg. (9 oz.) prepared angel food cake, cut into 1-inch cubes
- 3 fresh peaches, peeled, divided
- ¼ cup raspberry fruit spread
- 2 cups fresh raspberries, divided
- 2 pkg. (1 oz. each) JELL-O Vanilla Flavor Fat Free Sugar Free Instant Pudding
- 2½ cups fat-free milk
- 1½ cups thawed COOL WHIP LITE Whipped Topping, divided

▶ make it!

MIX orange juice and extract. Drizzle over cake cubes in large bowl; toss lightly. Cut 1 peach in half. Wrap 1 half tightly in plastic wrap; refrigerate until ready to use. Slice remaining peaches; place in medium bowl. Add fruit spread; mix lightly. Stir in 1 cup raspberries.

BEAT dry pudding mixes and milk in medium bowl with whisk 2 min. Stir in 1 cup COOL WHIP.

PLACE half the cake cubes in 2-qt. serving bowl or serving dish. Top with layers of half <u>each</u> of the peach mixture and pudding mixture. Top with remaining cake cubes, peach mixture and pudding mixture; cover. Refrigerate 2 hours. Top with remaining COOL WHIP just before serving. Peel and slice reserved peach half; arrange over dessert along with the remaining raspberries.

strawberry pretzel squares

PREP: 20 min. (plus baking and refrigerating) | **MAKES:** 20 servings.

▶ what you need!

2 cups finely crushed pretzels

½ cup sugar, divided

⅔ cup butter or margarine, melted

1½ pkg. (8 oz. each) PHILADELPHIA Cream Cheese, softened

2 Tbsp. milk

1 cup thawed COOL WHIP Whipped Topping

2 cups boiling water

1 pkg. (6 oz.) JELL-O Strawberry Flavor Gelatin

1½ cups cold water

4 cups fresh strawberries, sliced

▶ make it!

HEAT oven to 350°F.

MIX pretzel crumbs, ¼ cup of the sugar and the butter; press onto bottom of 13×9-inch baking pan. Bake 10 min. Cool.

BEAT cream cheese, remaining sugar and milk until well blended. Stir in COOL WHIP; spread over crust. Refrigerate.

ADD boiling water to dry gelatin mix in large bowl; stir 2 min. until completely dissolved. Stir in cold water. Refrigerate 1½ hours or until thickened.

STIR berries into gelatin; spoon over cream cheese layer. Refrigerate 3 hours or until firm.

MAKE IT EASY:
Substitute 1 pkg. (20 oz.) frozen whole strawberries, sliced, for the fresh strawberries. Stir into gelatin along with the cold water. Refrigerate 10 to 15 min. or until thickened, then spoon over cream cheese layer. Continue as directed.

triple-layer peanut butter brownies

PREP: 40 min. (plus refrigerating) | MAKES: 32 servings.

▸ what you need!

- 1 pkg. (19 to 21 oz.) brownie mix (13×9-inch pan size)
- 1 pkg. (3.4 oz.) JELL-O Vanilla Flavor Instant Pudding
- 1 cup cold milk
- 1 cup PLANTERS Creamy Peanut Butter
- ½ cup powdered sugar
- 1½ cups COOL WHIP Whipped Topping (Do not thaw.)
- 3 squares BAKER'S Semi-Sweet Chocolate
- ½ cup PLANTERS Dry Roasted Peanuts, coarsely chopped

▸ make it!

PREPARE and bake brownies in 13×9-inch pan as directed on package; cool. Meanwhile, beat dry pudding mix and milk with whisk 2 min. Add peanut butter and powdered sugar; mix well. Refrigerate until brownies are completely cooled.

SPREAD pudding mixture over brownies.

MICROWAVE COOL WHIP and chocolate on HIGH 1 min., stirring every 30 sec. Spread over pudding; top with nuts. Refrigerate 1 hour.

SUBSTITUTE:
Prepare using JELL-O White Chocolate Flavor Instant Pudding.

banana cream pie with caramel drizzle

PREP: 15 min. (plus refrigerating) | MAKES: 10 servings.

▶ what you need!

1½ bananas, divided

1 HONEY MAID Graham Pie Crust (6 oz.)

2 pkg. (3.4 oz. each) JELL-O Vanilla Flavor Instant Pudding

2 cups cold milk

2 cups thawed COOL WHIP Whipped Topping, divided

¼ cup caramel ice cream topping

▶ make it!

SLICE 1 of the bananas; spread onto bottom of crust.

BEAT dry pudding mixes and milk in medium bowl with whisk 2 min. Stir in 1 cup COOL WHIP. Pour into crust.

REFRIGERATE 4 hours or until firm. Drizzle with caramel topping just before serving. Top with remaining COOL WHIP and ½ banana. Store leftovers in refrigerator.

VARIATION:
Prepare as directed, using JELL-O Banana Cream Flavor Instant Pudding.

SUBSTITUTE:
Prepare using COOL WHIP LITE Whipped Topping.

14

cappuccino dessert

▸ what you need!

- 1 pkg. (1 oz.) JELL-O Vanilla Flavor Fat Free Sugar Free Instant Pudding
- 2 tsp. MAXWELL HOUSE Instant Coffee
- 2 cups cold fat-free milk
- ⅛ tsp. ground cinnamon
- 1 cup thawed COOL WHIP LITE Whipped Topping

▸ make it!

BEAT dry pudding mix, coffee granules and milk with whisk 2 min.; pour into 5 dessert dishes.

REFRIGERATE 1 hour.

MIX cinnamon into COOL WHIP. Spoon onto pudding.

No-Bake Delights

15

chocolate pudding pie

PREP: 15 min. (plus refrigerating) | MAKES: 10 servings.

▸ what you need!

1 pkg. (3.9 oz.) JELL-O Chocolate Instant Pudding

1½ cups cold milk

1 OREO Pie Crust (6 oz.)

2 cups thawed COOL WHIP Whipped Topping, divided

▸ make it!

BEAT dry pudding mix and milk with whisk 2 min.; spoon half into crust.

STIR 1 cup COOL WHIP into remaining pudding; spoon over pudding layer in crust.

TOP with remaining COOL WHIP. Refrigerate 3 hours.

SPECIAL EXTRA:
Sprinkle 2 Tbsp. chopped toasted PLANTERS Pecans onto bottom of crust before adding filling as directed.

cool 'n easy strawberry pie

▶ what you need!

2 cups fresh strawberries, divided

⅔ cup boiling water

1 pkg. (3 oz.) JELL-O Strawberry Flavor Gelatin

Ice cubes

½ cup cold water

1 tub (8 oz.) COOL WHIP LITE Whipped Topping, thawed

1 ready-to-use reduced-fat graham cracker crumb crust (6 oz.)

▶ make it!

SLICE 1 cup strawberries; refrigerate for later use. Chop remaining berries; set aside. Add boiling water to dry gelatin mix; stir 2 min. until completely dissolved. Add enough ice to cold water to make 1 cup. Add to gelatin; stir until slightly thickened. Remove any unmelted ice.

WHISK in COOL WHIP. Stir in chopped berries. Refrigerate 20 to 30 min. or until mixture is very thick and will mound. Spoon into crust.

REFRIGERATE 6 hours or until firm. Top with sliced berries.

SUBSTITUTE:
Prepare using COOL WHIP FREE Whipped Topping.

No-Bake Delights

easy tiramisu pie

PREP: 15 min. (plus refrigerating) | MAKES: 12 servings.

▸ what you need!

48 NILLA Wafers, divided

¼ cup brewed strong
MAXWELL HOUSE Coffee,
cooled, divided

4 oz. (½ of 8-oz. pkg.)
PHILADELPHIA Cream
Cheese, softened

1½ cups cold milk

1 pkg. (3.4 oz.) JELL-O Vanilla Flavor Instant Pudding

2 cups thawed COOL WHIP Season's Delight French Vanilla
Whipped Topping or COOL WHIP Whipped Topping

1 square BAKER'S Semi-Sweet Chocolate, grated

▸ make it!

ARRANGE 36 wafers on bottom and up side of 9-inch pie plate. Drizzle
with 2 Tbsp. coffee.

BEAT cream cheese in large bowl with mixer until creamy. Gradually
beat in milk. Add dry pudding mix; beat 1 min. Gently stir in COOL
WHIP.

LAYER half each of the pudding mixture and grated chocolate in crust;
cover with remaining wafers. Drizzle with remaining coffee. Repeat
layers of pudding and chocolate. Refrigerate 3 hours.

HOW TO SOFTEN CREAM CHEESE:
Place measured amount of cream cheese in microwaveable bowl. Microwave
on HIGH 10 sec. or until slightly softened.

frozen raspberry shortcake squares

PREP: 10 min. (plus freezing) | **MAKES:** 12 servings, 1 square each.

▶ what you need!

2 cups frozen raspberry nonfat yogurt, softened

1 pkg. (0.3 oz.) JELL-O Raspberry Flavor Sugar Free Gelatin

1 tub (8 oz.) COOL WHIP Sugar Free Whipped Topping, thawed

1 pkg. (10.75 oz.) prepared reduced-fat pound cake, cubed

▶ make it!

WHISK yogurt and dry gelatin mix in large bowl until well blended. Stir in COOL WHIP. Add cake cubes; mix lightly.

SPOON into 8-inch square pan.

FREEZE 3 hours or until firm.

SUBSTITUTE:
Prepare using COOL WHIP LITE Whipped Topping.

VARIATION:
Prepare using frozen strawberry nonfat yogurt and JELL-O Strawberry Flavor Sugar Free Gelatin.

No-Bake Delights

raspberry angel cake

▶ what you need!

3 cups boiling water

2 pkg. (3 oz. each) JELL-O Raspberry Flavor Gelatin

1 pkg. (12 oz.) frozen red raspberries (Do not thaw.)

1 pkg. (7.5 oz.) round angel food cake, cut into 21 thin slices

1 cup thawed COOL WHIP Whipped Topping

▶ make it!

ADD boiling water to dry gelatin mixes in medium bowl; stir 2 min. until completely dissolved. Add raspberries; stir until thawed. Pour into 9-inch round pan sprayed with cooking spray.

ARRANGE cake slices in concentric circles over gelatin, with slices overlapping as necessary to completely cover gelatin.

REFRIGERATE 3 hours or until gelatin is firm. Unmold onto plate; top with COOL WHIP.

HOW TO UNMOLD DESSERT:
Dip knife in warm water and run knife around edge of chilled dessert to loosen. Dip pan in warm water, just to rim, for 15 sec. Lift from water and gently pull gelatin from edge of pan with moistened fingers. Place serving plate on top of pan. Invert pan and plate and shake to loosen dessert. Gently remove pan.

SPECIAL EXTRA:
Garnish with fresh raspberries and mint leaves.

No-Bake Delights

20

creamy pudding sauce

PREP: 5 min. | **MAKES:** 24 servings, 2 Tbsp. each.

▶ what you need!

1 pkg. (1 oz.) JELL-O Vanilla
Flavor Fat Free Sugar Free
Instant Pudding

¼ tsp. ground cinnamon

3 cups cold fat-free milk

▶ make it!

BEAT ingredients with whisk 2 min.

NOTE:
Drizzle sauce over a slice of warm pie.

SAUCE SWIRLS & HEARTS:
Spoon sauce onto individual dessert plates. Drop small amounts of another
dessert sauce, melted chocolate, or strawberry or raspberry jelly, from spoon
at intervals over sauce near rim of plate. Swirl with toothpick. Or, pull through
the drops of sauce, connecting each drop, around the entire plate, to create a
heart-shaped design. Top with one serving of cake, pie, brownie or cheesecake.

No-Bake Delights

21

beautifully easy fruit tart

PREP: 15 min. (plus baking and cooling) | MAKES: 9 servings.

▸ what you need!

- 1 sheet frozen puff pastry (½ of 17.3-oz. pkg.), thawed
- 1 pkg. (3.4 oz.) JELL-O Vanilla Flavor Instant Pudding
- 1 cup cold milk
- 1 cup thawed COOL WHIP Whipped Topping
- 1 square BAKER'S White Chocolate
- 1 cup quartered fresh strawberries
- 1 can (11 oz.) mandarin oranges, drained
- 1 kiwi, peeled, sliced and halved
- 3 Tbsp. apricot preserves
- 2 tsp. water

▸ make it!

HEAT oven to 400°F.

UNROLL pastry on baking sheet. Fold over edges of pastry to form ½-inch rim; press together firmly to seal. Prick pastry sheet with fork. Bake 10 to 15 min. or until puffed and golden brown. Cool completely. Place on tray.

BEAT dry pudding mix and milk in large bowl with whisk 2 min. Stir in COOL WHIP; spread onto pastry.

MELT chocolate as directed on package. Arrange fruit over pudding mixture. Mix preserves and water; brush onto fruit. Drizzle with chocolate. Let stand until chocolate is firm.

HOW TO DRIZZLE CHOCOLATE:
Dip a large spoon into the bowl of melted chocolate. Quickly move the spoon back and forth over the tart, letting the chocolate fall in thin ribbons from the end of the spoon. Repeat until all of the chocolate is used.

SUBSTITUTE:
Substitute orange marmalade or pineapple preserves for the apricot preserves.

cranberry-pineapple minis

▸ what you need!

- 1 can (20 oz.) crushed pineapple, in juice, undrained
- 2 pkg. (3 oz. each) JELL-O Raspberry Flavor Gelatin
- 1 can (16 oz.) whole berry cranberry sauce
- ⅔ cup chopped PLANTERS Walnuts
- 1 apple, chopped

▸ make it!

DRAIN pineapple, reserving juice. Add enough water to reserved juice to measure 2½ cups; pour into saucepan. Bring to boil. Add to dry gelatin mixes in large bowl; stir 2 min. until completely dissolved.

STIR in pineapple, cranberry sauce, nuts and apples. Spoon into 24 paper-lined muffin cups.

REFRIGERATE 2½ hours or until firm. Remove desserts from liners before serving.

SUBSTITUTE:
Prepare using JELL-O Cherry Flavor Gelatin or JELL-O Raspberry Flavor Sugar Free Gelatin.

Fruit Frenzy

23

creamy layered peach squares

PREP: 30 min. (plus refrigerating) | MAKES: 20 servings.

▸ what you need!

2 cups HONEY MAID Graham Cracker Crumbs

½ cup sugar, divided

½ cup butter or margarine, melted

1½ pkg. (8 oz. each) PHILADELPHIA Cream Cheese, softened

1 tub (8 oz.) COOL WHIP Whipped Topping, thawed, divided

3 large fresh peaches (about 1¼ lb.), peeled, sliced

1½ cups boiling water

1 pkg. (6 oz.) JELL-O Raspberry Flavor Gelatin

2 cups ice cubes

▸ make it!

MIX graham crumbs, ¼ cup sugar and butter in 13×9-inch pan; press onto bottom of pan.

BEAT cream cheese and remaining sugar in medium bowl until well blended. Whisk in 1½ cups COOL WHIP; spread over crust. Top with peaches. Refrigerate until ready to use.

ADD boiling water to dry gelatin mix in large bowl; stir 2 min. until completely dissolved. Stir in ice cubes until melted. Refrigerate 5 min. or until thickened. Whisk in remaining COOL WHIP; spread over peach layer. Refrigerate 4 hours or until firm.

SPECIAL EXTRA:
Garnish with fresh raspberries and peach slices.

layered strawberry cheesecake bowl

PREP: 20 min. (plus refrigerating) | **MAKES:** 14 servings, ⅔ cup each.

▶ what you need!

- 3 cups sliced fresh strawberries
- 3 Tbsp. sugar
- 2 pkg. (8 oz. each) PHILADELPHIA Neufchâtel Cheese, softened
- 1½ cups cold milk
- 1 pkg. (3.4 oz.) JELL-O Vanilla Flavor Instant Pudding
- 2 cups thawed COOL WHIP LITE Whipped Topping, divided
- 2 cups frozen pound cake cubes (1 inch)
- 1 square BAKER'S Semi-Sweet Chocolate

▶ make it!

COMBINE berries and sugar; refrigerate until ready to use. Beat Neufchâtel with mixer until creamy. Gradually beat in milk. Add dry pudding mix; mix well.

BLEND in 1½ cups COOL WHIP. Spoon half into 2½-qt. serving bowl.

TOP with layers of cake, berries and remaining Neufchâtel mixture. Refrigerate 4 hours.

MELT chocolate; drizzle over trifle. Top with remaining CCOL WHIP.

SPECIAL EXTRA:
Garnish with a chocolate-dipped strawberry just before serving.

NOTE:
You will need about half of a 10.75-oz. pkg. pound cake to get the 2 cups cake cubes needed to prepare this recipe.

Fruit Frenzy

"sangria" fruit cups

PREP: 20 min. (plus refrigerating) | MAKES: 8 servings, about ½ cup each.

▶ what you need!

1 cup orange juice

1 pkg. (3 oz.) JELL-O Strawberry Flavor Gelatin

1 pkg. (3 oz.) JELL-O Lemon Flavor Gelatin

1½ cups cold water

1 cup pitted fresh sweet cherries, halved

8 strawberries, quartered

1 nectarine, peeled and sliced

1 cup thawed COOL WHIP Whipped Topping

▶ make it!

BRING orange juice to boil. Add to dry gelatin mixes in medium bowl; stir 2 min. until completely dissolved. Stir in cold water.

SPOON fruit into 8 clear cups. Cover with gelatin mixture.

REFRIGERATE 4 hours or until firm. Top with COOL WHIP just before serving.

SUBSTITUTE:
Substitute seedless grape halves for the cherries.

VARIATION:
Prepare using your favorite flavor JELL-O Gelatin.

simply sensational strawberry shortcake

PREP: 20 min. (plus baking and cooling) | MAKES: 8 servings.

▶ what you need!

- 1¼ cups milk, divided
- ¼ cup BREAKSTONE'S or KNUDSEN Sour Cream
- 3 Tbsp. sugar
- 2¼ cups all-purpose baking mix
- 1 pkg. (3.4 oz.) JELL-O Vanilla Flavor Instant Pudding
- 1 tub (8 oz.) COOL WHIP Whipped Topping, thawed, divided
- 4 cups sliced fresh strawberries
- ⅓ cup sugar

▶ make it!

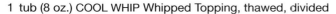

HEAT oven to 425°F.

BEAT ½ cup milk, sour cream and 3 Tbsp. sugar in large bowl with whisk until well blended. Stir in baking mix just until moistened. Spread onto bottom of greased 9-inch round pan. Bake 12 to 15 min. or until golden brown. Cool 10 min.; remove to wire rack. Cool completely.

BEAT dry pudding mix and remaining milk in medium bowl with whisk 2 min. Stir in half the COOL WHIP. Toss strawberries with ⅓ cup sugar.

CUT cake horizontally in half; stack layers on plate, filling with half the strawberry mixture and all the pudding mixture. Top with remaining COOL WHIP and strawberry mixture. Serve immediately.

SUBSTITUTE:
Substitute 2 pkg. (10 oz. each) frozen sliced strawberries for the fresh strawberries.

Fruit Frenzy

triple strawberry no-drip pops

PREP: 10 min. (plus freezing) | MAKES: 8 servings.

▸ what you need!

2 cups boiling water

1 pkg. (3 oz.) JELL-O Strawberry Flavor Gelatin

18 fresh strawberries, stemmed

⅔ cup (filled to 2-qt. line) KOOL-AID Strawberry Flavor Sugar-Sweetened Soft Drink Mix, or any red flavor

▸ make it!

ADD boiling water to dry gelatin mix; stir 2 min. until completely dissolved.

CUT strawberries in half. Mash berries and drink mix in large bowl with fork. Stir in gelatin.

POUR into 8 (5-oz.) paper cups.

COVER cups with foil, insert wooden pop stick into center of each for handle. Freeze 2 hours or until firm.

VARIATION TWIST ON YOUR POP FLAVOR!:
Mix and match this refreshing summer pop with your favorite flavor combination of JELL-O, KOOL-AID and fruit.

MAKE AHEAD:
Make ahead to have on hand for an "anytime" snack.

chocolate-cherry pie

PREP: 15 min. (plus refrigerating) | **MAKES:** 8 servings.

▸ what you need!

- 1 can (21 oz.) cherry pie filling, divided
- 1 HONEY MAID Graham Pie Crust (6 oz.)
- 2 pkg. (3.9 oz. each) JELL-O Chocolate Instant Pudding
- 1½ cups cold milk
- 2½ cups thawed COOL WHIP Whipped Topping, divided

▸ make it!

SPREAD 1 cup cherry pie filling onto bottom of crust. Beat dry pudding mixes and milk in medium bowl with whisk 2 min. Stir in 1½ cups COOL WHIP; spread over cherry layer in crust.

SPOON remaining COOL WHIP around edge of pie to form 1-inch border. Fill center with remaining cherry pie filling.

REFRIGERATE 4 hours or until firm.

HOW TO THAW COOL WHIP WHIPPED TOPPING:

The best way to thaw frozen COOL WHIP Whipped Topping is in its container in the refrigerator. Depending on the size tub you have, the thawing time varies. Recommended thawing times are: 8-oz. tub: 4 hours; 12-oz. tub: 5 hours; 16-oz. tub: 6 hours. We DO NOT recommend thawing COOL WHIP Whipped Topping in the microwave.

Fruit Frenzy

29

easy autumn pear cake

PREP: 15 min. (plus baking) | MAKES: 24 servings.

▶ what you need!

4 oz. (½ of 8-oz. pkg.) PHILADELPHIA Cream Cheese, softened

½ cup BREAKSTONE'S or KNUDSEN Sour Cream

1 egg

1 pkg. (2-layer size) yellow cake mix

7 Tbsp. butter, melted, divided

1 can (15 oz.) pear halves, drained, cut into ½-inch-thick slices

1 pkg. (3 oz.) JELL-O Lemon Flavor Gelatin

½ tsp. ground cinnamon

½ cup chopped PLANTERS Walnuts

▶ make it!

HEAT oven to 350°F.

BEAT first 4 ingredients in large bowl with mixer on low speed just until cake mix is moistened, stopping frequently to scrape side of bowl. Add ¼ cup butter; beat on medium speed 2 min. (Batter will be thick.)

SPREAD batter onto bottom of 13×9-inch pan sprayed with cooking spray. Arrange pear slices over batter, pressing lightly into batter to secure. Sprinkle with dry gelatin mix and cinnamon. Drizzle with remaining butter; sprinkle with nuts.

BAKE 40 to 45 min. or until toothpick inserted in center comes out clean.

SUBSTITUTE:
Prepare using a lemon or spice cake mix.

banana bread minis

PREP: 15 min. (plus baking) | MAKES: 20 servings or 5 loaves, 4 servings each.

▸ what you need!

1 pkg. (2-layer size) yellow cake mix

1 pkg. (3.4 oz.) JELL-O Banana Cream Flavor Instant Pudding

4 eggs

1 cup water

¼ cup oil

1 cup mashed fully ripe bananas (about 3)

½ cup chopped PLANTERS Walnuts

▸ make it!

HEAT oven to 350°F.

BEAT first 5 ingredients in large bowl with mixer 2 min. or until well blended. Add bananas and nuts; mix just until blended.

POUR into 5 foil mini loaf pans sprayed with cooking spray.

BAKE 40 min. or until toothpick inserted in centers comes out clean. Cool completely.

SUBSTITUTE:
Prepare using JELL-O Vanilla Flavor Instant Pudding.

HOW TO STORE RIPE BANANAS:
Have too many ripe bananas? Mash bananas, then store 1-cup portions in separate resealable freezer bags. Freeze up to 3 months. Thaw in refrigerator before using to prepare these delicious banana breads.

Fruit Frenzy

JELL-O Holiday JIGGLERS

▸ what you need!

2½ cups boiling water

4 pkg. (3 oz. each) JELL-O Gelatin

▸ make it!

ADD boiling water to dry gelatin mixes; stir 3 min. until completely dissolved.

POUR into 13×9-inch pan. Refrigerate 3 hours or until firm.

DIP bottom of pan in warm water 15 sec. Cut gelatin into shapes using JELL-O Holiday JIGGLERS Cutters.

KEEP KIDS SAFE:
For children under 6 years of age, cut JIGGLERS into small bite-size pieces. Children should always be seated and supervised while eating. For more information, visit www.KraftKidsSafe.com.

irish cream chocolate mousse

PREP: 10 min. (plus refrigerating) | **MAKES:** 6 servings, ½ cup each.

▶ what you need!

1 pkg. (3.9 oz.) JELL-O
  Chocolate Instant Pudding

1¼ cups cold milk

¼ cup Irish cream liqueur

2 cups thawed COOL WHIP
  Whipped Topping, divided

½ cup fresh raspberries

▶ make it!

BEAT dry pudding mix, milk and liqueur in medium bowl with whisk 2 min. Stir in 1½ cups COOL WHIP.

SPOON into dessert dishes. Refrigerate 20 min.

TOP with remaining COOL WHIP and berries.

SPECIAL EXTRA:
Top with grated BAKER'S Semi-Sweet Chocolate.

Seasonal Desserts

33

summer berry pie

PREP: 25 min. (plus refrigerating) | MAKES: 10 servings.

▸ what you need!

¾ cup sugar

3 Tbsp. cornstarch

1½ cups water

1 pkg. (3 oz.) JELL-O Strawberry Flavor Gelatin

1 cup each: blueberries, raspberries and sliced strawberries

1 HONEY MAID Graham Pie Crust (6 oz.)

1½ cups thawed COOL WHIP Whipped Topping

▸ make it!

MIX sugar and cornstarch in medium saucepan. Gradually add water, stirring until well blended. Bring to boil on medium heat, stirring constantly; boil 1 min. Remove from heat. Add dry gelatin mix; stir until dissolved. Stir in fruit.

POUR into crust.

REFRIGERATE 3 hours or until firm. Top with COOL WHIP just before serving. Store any leftover pie in refrigerator.

SPECIAL EXTRA:
For a great summer cooler, serve topped with scoops of vanilla ice cream instead of the COOL WHIP.

patriotic fruit pizza

PREP: 20 min. | MAKES: 16 servings.

▶ what you need!

- 1 pkg. (16.5 oz.) refrigerated sliceable sugar cookies, sliced
- 1 pkg. (3.4 oz.) JELL-O Vanilla Flavor Instant Pudding
- 1¼ cups cold milk
- 3 cups JET-PUFFED Miniature Marshmallows, divided
- 1 cup thawed COOL WHIP Whipped Topping
- 2 cups cut-up fresh fruit, such as strawberries, raspberries and blueberries

▶ make it!

HEAT oven to 350°F.

LINE 12-inch pizza pan with foil; spray with cooking spray. Arrange dough slices in pan; press together to form crust. Bake 14 to 16 min. or until lightly browned. Cool completely. Remove cookie from pan and foil; place on plate.

BEAT dry pudding mix and milk in large bowl with whisk 2 min. Let stand 5 min. Stir in 2 cups marshmallows and COOL WHIP; spread onto crust.

TOP with fruit and remaining marshmallows.

SUBSTITUTE:
Substitute other fruits, such as seedless grapes, orange sections, banana slices and/or peeled kiwi slices for the strawberries, raspberries and blueberries.

VARIATION:
If pizza pan is not available, trace a 12-inch circle on parchment paper or foil; place on baking sheet. Press cookie dough onto circle. Bake as directed.

Seasonal Desserts

turtle pumpkin pie

PREP: 15 min. (plus refrigerating) | MAKES: 10 servings.

▶ what you need!

- ¼ cup plus 2 Tbsp. caramel ice cream topping, divided
- 1 HONEY MAID Graham Pie Crust (6 oz.)
- ½ cup plus 2 Tbsp. chopped PLANTERS Pecans, divided
- 2 pkg. (3.4 oz. each) JELL-O Vanilla Flavor Instant Pudding
- 1 cup cold milk
- 1 cup canned pumpkin
- 1 tsp. ground cinnamon
- ½ tsp. ground nutmeg
- 1 tub (8 oz.) COOL WHIP Whipped Topping, thawed, divided

▶ make it!

POUR ¼ cup caramel topping into crust; sprinkle with ½ cup nuts.

BEAT dry pudding mixes, milk, pumpkin and spices with whisk until blended. Stir in 1½ cups COOL WHIP. Spoon into crust.

REFRIGERATE 1 hour. Top with remaining COOL WHIP, 2 Tbsp. caramel topping and nuts just before serving.

JELL-O easy patriotic pie

PREP: 20 min. (plus refrigerating) | **MAKES:** 8 servings.

▶ what you need!

1½ cups boiling water, divided

1 pkg. (3 oz.) JELL-O Berry Blue Flavor Gelatin

1 cup ice cubes, divided

1 HONEY MAID Graham Pie Crust (6 oz.)

1 pkg. (3 oz.) JELL-O Strawberry Flavor Gelatin, or any red flavor

1 cup thawed COOL WHIP Whipped Topping

▶ make it!

ADD ¾ cup boiling water to blue gelatin mix; stir 2 min. until completely dissolved. Add ½ cup ice cubes; stir until melted. Pour into crust; refrigerate 5 to 10 min. or until set but not firm.

MEANWHILE, repeat to dissolve red gelatin mix in separate bowl; stir in remaining ice cubes. Cool 5 min. or until slightly thickened.

SPREAD COOL WHIP over blue gelatin layer; cover with red gelatin. Refrigerate 2 hours or until set.

BEST OF SEASON:

Garnish with fresh seasonal berries just before serving. Or, arrange ½ cup berries on bottom of pie crust before covering with the blue gelatin.

VARIATION:

Prepare as directed, using your favorite 2 flavors of JELL-O Gelatin.

Seasonal Desserts

easy holiday ribbon bowl

PREP: 15 min. (plus refrigerating) | **MAKES:** 8 servings, ½ cup each.

▶ what you need!

2¼ cups boiling water, divided

1 pkg. (3 oz.) JELL-O Lime Flavor Gelatin

1 cup ice cubes

1 pkg. (3 oz.) JELL-O Strawberry Flavor Gelatin

1 tub (8 oz.) COOL WHIP Whipped Topping (Do not thaw.), divided

▶ make it!

ADD ¾ cup boiling water to lime gelatin mix in medium bowl; stir 2 min. until completely dissolved. Add ice; stir until gelatin is slightly thickened. Remove any unmelted ice. Pour gelatin into 1- to 1½-qt. bowl. Refrigerate 15 min. or until set but not firm.

ADD remaining boiling water to strawberry gelatin mix in large bowl; stir 2 min. until completely dissolved. Add ⅔ of the COOL WHIP; stir with whisk until COOL WHIP is melted and mixture is well blended. Refrigerate remaining COOL WHIP for later use. Carefully spoon strawberry gelatin mixture over lime gelatin layer.

REFRIGERATE 2 hours or until set. Top with remaining COOL WHIP just before serving.

MAKE IT EASY:
No need to thaw the COOL WHIP. By using frozen COOL WHIP, the dessert magically layers right before your eyes.

red and green holiday mold

PREP: 20 min. (plus refrigerating) | **MAKES:** 10 servings, ½ cup each.

▸ what you need!

2½ cups boiling water, divided

1 pkg. (6 oz.) JELL-O Gelatin, any red flavor

1 cup cold water

1 pkg. (3 oz.) JELL-O Lime Flavor Gelatin

1 cup vanilla ice cream, softened

½ cup thawed COOL WHIP Whipped Topping

▸ make it!

ADD 1½ cups boiling water to red gelatin mix in large bowl; stir 2 min. until completely dissolved. Stir in cold water. Reserve 1½ cups gelatin; let stand at room temperature. Pour remaining gelatin into 5-cup mold sprayed with cooking spray. Refrigerate 45 min. or until set but not firm.

STIR remaining boiling water into lime gelatin mix in medium bowl 2 min. until completely dissolved. Add ice cream; stir until completely melted. Spoon over red gelatin layer in mold. Refrigerate 20 min. or until gelatin is set but not firm.

SPOON reserved red gelatin over creamy layer in mold. Refrigerate 4 hours or until firm. Unmold. Top with COOL WHIP.

VARIATION:
Prepare using JELL-O Sugar Free Gelatin, frozen low-fat vanilla yogurt and COOL WHIP LITE Whipped Topping.

HOW TO UNMOLD GELATIN:
Dip mold in warm water for about 15 sec. Gently pull gelatin from around edge with moist fingers. Place moistened serving plate on top of mold. Invert mold and plate; holding mold and plate together, shake slightly to loosen. Gently remove mold and center gelatin on plate.

Seasonal Desserts

39

aquarium cups

▶ what you need!

¾ cup boiling water

1 pkg. (3 oz.) JELL-O Berry Blue Flavor Gelatin

Ice cubes

½ cup cold water

½ cup chopped strawberries

4 bite-size fish-shaped chewy fruit snacks

▶ make it!

ADD boiling water to gelatin in medium bowl; stir 2 min. until completely dissolved. Add enough ice cubes to cold water to measure 1¼ cups. Add to gelatin; stir until slightly thickened. Remove any unmelted ice. If gelatin is still thin, refrigerate until slightly thickened.

PLACE berries in 4 clear plastic cups; cover with gelatin. Press fruit snacks into gelatin until completely submerged.

REFRIGERATE 1 hour or until firm.

SUBSTITUTE:
Substitute your favorite fruit for the strawberries.

chocolate-peanut butter candy dessert

PREP: 15 min. (plus refrigerating) | **MAKES:** 12 servings.

▸ what you need!

- 12 OREO Cookies, crushed
- 2 Tbsp. butter, melted
- 2 cups cold milk
- ½ cup PLANTERS Creamy Peanut Butter
- 2 pkg. (3.9 oz. each) JELL-O Chocolate Instant Pudding
- 2 cups thawed COOL WHIP Whipped Topping, divided
- 2 Tbsp. hot fudge ice cream topping
- ¼ cup candy-coated peanut butter pieces

▸ make it!

MIX crushed cookies and butter; press onto bottom of 8-inch square pan.

ADD milk gradually to peanut butter in large bowl, stirring with whisk until well blended. Add dry pudding mixes; beat 2 min. (Mixture will be thick.) Stir in 1 cup COOL WHIP. Spread onto crust; cover with remaining COOL WHIP.

REFRIGERATE 3 hours or until firm. When ready to serve, microwave fudge topping as directed on label; drizzle over dessert. Top with peanut butter pieces.

MAKE AHEAD:
Make this dessert the day before the party and keep in the refrigerator until ready to serve.

dirt cups

PREP: 15 min. (plus refrigerating) | MAKES: 10 servings.

▸ what you need!

- 1 pkg. (3.9 oz.) JELL-O Chocolate Instant Pudding
- 2 cups cold milk
- 1 tub (8 oz.) COOL WHIP Whipped Topping, thawed
- 15 OREO Cookies, finely crushed (about 1¼ cups), divided
- 10 worm-shaped chewy fruit snacks

▸ make it!

BEAT dry pudding mix and milk in large bowl with whisk 2 min. Let stand 5 min. Stir in COOL WHIP and ½ cup cookie crumbs.

SPOON into 10 (6- to 7-oz.) plastic or paper cups; top with remaining cookie crumbs.

REFRIGERATE 1 hour. Top with fruit snacks just before serving.

SAND CUPS:
Prepare using JELL-O Vanilla Flavor Instant Pudding and 35 NILLA Wafers.

double-chocolate mousse

PREP: 10 min. (plus refrigerating) | MAKES: 6 servings.

▶ what you need!

- 1½ cups fat-free milk, divided
- 2 squares BAKER'S Semi-Sweet Chocolate
- 1 pkg. (2.1 oz.) JELL-O Chocolate Fat Free Sugar Free Instant Pudding
- 2 cups thawed COOL WHIP FREE Whipped Topping, divided
- ½ cup fresh raspberries

▶ make it!

MICROWAVE 1 cup milk and chocolate squares in large microwaveable bowl on HIGH 2 min.; whisk until chocolate is melted. Add remaining milk and dry pudding mix; beat 2 min. Refrigerate 20 min.

WHISK in 1½ cups COOL WHIP; spoon into 6 dessert dishes.

TOP with remaining COOL WHIP. Garnish with berries.

Kid Favorites

easy banana pudding parfaits

PREP: 15 min. (plus refrigerating) | MAKES: 2 servings.

▸ what you need!

12 NILLA Wafers, divided

¼ cup thawed COOL WHIP Whipped Topping, divided

1 small banana, cut into 10 slices, divided

2 JELL-O Vanilla Pudding Snacks

▸ make it!

CRUSH 10 wafers to form coarse crumbs; place ¼ of the crumbs in each of 2 parfait glasses. Top each with 1 Tbsp. COOL WHIP, 2 banana slices and half of 1 pudding snack. Repeat layers of crumbs, bananas and pudding.

REFRIGERATE 15 min. Meanwhile, wrap reserved banana slices tightly in plastic wrap; refrigerate until ready to use.

TOP parfaits with remaining COOL WHIP, wafers and banana slices just before serving.

HOW TO PREVENT THE BANANA SLICES FROM TURNING BROWN:
Toss banana slices with small amount of lemon juice.

snowman cups

PREP: 15 min. | MAKES: 10 servings, ½ cup each.

▶ what you need!

- 2 pkg. (3.9 oz. each) JELL-O Chocolate Instant Pudding
- 1 qt. (4 cups) cold milk
- 20 OREO Cookies, crushed (about 2 cups), divided
- 2 cups thawed COOL WHIP Whipped Topping

  Assorted decorating gels

▶ make it!

BEAT dry pudding mixes and milk with whisk 2 min. Let stand 5 min. Stir in 1 cup cookie crumbs.

SPOON remaining cookie crumbs into 10 (6- to 7-oz.) plastic cups; cover with pudding mixture.

DROP spoonfuls of COOL WHIP onto desserts to resemble snowmen. Decorate with gels for the eyes, noses and scarves.

MAKE IT EASY:
Instead of dropping spoonfuls of the COOL WHIP onto desserts, fill resealable plastic bag with COOL WHIP; seal bag. Using scissors, diagonally snip off 1 corner from bottom of bag. Squeeze COOL WHIP from bag to create snowmen. Decorate as directed.

Kid Favorites

45

strawberry snow cones

▶ what you need!

- 1 cup boiling water
- 1 pkg. (6 oz.) JELL-O Gelatin, any red flavor
- 1 cup puréed strawberries
- ½ cup light corn syrup
- ½ cup ice cubes
- 8 cups crushed ice

▶ make it!

ADD boiling water to dry gelatin mix in large bowl; stir 2 min. until completely dissolved. Add strawberries, corn syrup and ice cubes; stir until ice is completely melted.

SPOON crushed ice into 8 (8-oz.) paper or plastic cups.

SPOON gelatin mixture over ice. Serve immediately.

FUN IDEA:
Let the kids make their own holders for the prepared snow cones. Use markers to decorate sheets of construction paper. Roll up each to form cone shape; secure with staples. Insert filled paper cups into holders just before serving.

STORAGE KNOW-HOW:
If you have more snow cones than kids, wrap filled cups well with plastic wrap; store in freezer up to 3 weeks. Remove from freezer about 5 min. before serving.

Kid Favorites